My Very First Book
of
Numbers & Colors

My Very First Book
of
Numbers & Colors

Jeanetta Varney Kozey

authorHOUSE®

AuthorHouse™ LLC
1663 Liberty Drive
Bloomington, IN 47403
www.authorhouse.com
Phone: 1-800-839-8640

Published by AuthorHouse   01/14/2014

ISBN: 978-1-4918-4095-5 (sc)

My
First book of numbers

Written & Illustrated by:
Jeanetta R. Kozey

My First Book of

Numbers

According to the Bible

This Book belongs

to: _____

One tells us that
there is only one God
and he will have no
others before him.

Two

2

Two tells us that
there are two
sections to the
bible.
The Old Testament and
the New Testament
Also God is with me
always

Three

3

This tells us of the Father, Son, and Holy Spirit. People call this the Trinity.

Four

The number4 tells us
about the 4 corners
of the world.
 Jesus tells us to go
  to the uttermost
parts of the world to
 tell people of what
he has done for them.

Five

5

The number 5 tells us
about the full
ministry gifts known
as Preacher,Teacher
Apostle,
Evangelist,and
Prophet
It tells of his full
power.

Six

The number 6 tells us that on the 6th day of creation he made man and it is the number of man.

Seven

7

The number seven
tells us that on the
7th day God rested
after creating all
that was and is
today.

Seven

Eight

8

Eight is used to tell
us of the spiritual
birthing inside of
man. All mankind
will birth a reality
of what God's word
means.

Nine

Nine is a very
important number;
just ask any mother.
It takes 9 months for
most babies to be
fully formed and
ready to be born.

The number 10 tells
us of all that God
is, 'became' visible
at this time. We
would have to start
over after every ten
numbers we start at
one again.

Ten

Remember Kids,
What you believe
You can achieve!

The Adventures of Bible Bob

Catalog of Books

1. Bible Bob Goes in Search of the Zoo
2. Bible Bob Goes Fishing
3. Bible Bob Goes Mountain Climbing
4. Bible Bob Goes to a Wrestling Match
5. Bible Bob Goes Camping
6. Bible Bob Goes on a Picnic
7. Bible Bob Goes Horseback Riding
8. Bible Bob Goes to a Parade
9. Bible Bob Finds the Chief Cornerstone
10. Bible Bob Hangs Around a Cross
11. Will the Real God Please Stand Up?
12. Bible Bob's Grandpa Comes for a Visit
13. Bible Bob Talks a New Talk
14. What Kind of Coat are you Wearing?

My Very own Book of Colors

(According to the bible)

Written by: Jeanetta Varney Kozey

The way I remember my colors is by the name

ROY G. BIV

R stands for red:

Which means the color of Jesus blood

Jesus shed His blood on the cross for you and me.

O stands for orange:

It takes red and yellow to make orange.

Red= blood

Yellow= God's glory. Look around you
and you see God's glory shining all day.

So mix the two together and you get
orange.

Yellow = God's glory. Look
around you and you can see all of God's
glory in the sunshine…

G=green.

It stands for eternal life. That is why we
have evergreens. They are evergreen.
It also stands for the Holy Spirit, which
teaches us.

B=blue

This is the color of water. Also water
stands for the word of God.

I= indigo

Which is a color of purple. It stands for his royalty.

V=violet

Is a word for purple; which is his

royalty.   He had a robe of purple when
he was hanged on the cross.

There are 2 other colors that we need to 'talk' about.

White = purity or righteousness.

We have been given the robe of righteousness.

Black = darkness or sin as most people talk about it.
It can also mean wilderness as we walk around not knowing what or why we are doing what we do…

That just about does it for our colors. I hope you enjoyed this visit with Bible Bob.

See you next time!

Your friend,

Bible Bob

Bible Bob

Printed in the United States
By Bookmasters